Publisher : Linear Structure Press
Cover Design : The Chad Barr Group

9/11/18

To Bernhard

Here's to your continued
Success!

Best Regards.
Peter.

CONTENTS PAGE

INTRODUCTION

I believe globally there are thousands of high-potential sales managers who despite being highly motivated to succeed are nevertheless struggling to survive.

They are ready and willing to do the right thing. What they lack is help and advice on what to do.

My heartfelt desire is to help fill this need and provide practical specifics for creating sustainable success in sales management.

Too often great sales people get the promotion to manager with distastrous results for everyone concerned. Fundamentally, these are two different skills.

Smart companies and management recognize this fact and invest in developing their sales managers, a key element in creating a sustainable high-performance sales culture.

I wish you much success in applying these principles within your organisation and transforming both your own results and the value you create for your clients.

Peter Holland

ACKNOWLEDGEMENT PAGE

Firstly, I'd like to thank my wife Carole for her daily support, encouragement and valued objectivity! And our children, Raphael and Laeticia, for their daily lessons of inspiration and creativity which remind me to take a fresh perspective.

This book would just be hypothetical theory without the opportunity to work together with some amazing clients. So I want to thank: Tony Butler, Richard McDonald, Ian Rose, John Kerr, Graham Taylor, Simon & Sarah Herman, Helen Emanuelsson, Mathias Ehrenstrom, Eva Carin Mattsson and Tony Browne. It's been a pleasure working with you all, and having the opportunity to create results in real life!

As with any new endeavour, we need mentors to succeed and I'm very grateful to Alan Weiss and Stuart Cross for their wise advice. And especially Chad Barr for his digital expertise and ongoing encouragement to write this book together with his amazing team for their design talents in bringing it to life.

CHAPTER 1.

A Brief History of Sales

Where we've been, where we're at and where we're going!

Or.... Why your past results are no guarantee of future success.

Are you staying relevant in your customer's eyes?

We are living through a period of rapid change in the sales environment. Many senior sales professionals are discovering their old sales approaches are no longer delivering results, causing them to see their valuable careers running off the rails. Change and adaptation are vital in today's sales world.

Change and adaptation are vital in today's sales world.

THE ONLY CONSTANT IN LIFE IS CHANGE

Discovering the specific attributes your customers truly value is the key to your sales success.

If you've been involved in the sales industry for any length of time, chances are you will have been exposed to several different and, at times, complex sales methodologies. Starting way back in the 1960's, Xerox developed their "Needs Satisfaction" approach improving selling significantly, which also influenced Neil Rackham's popular book Spin Selling. In the meantime, Bob Miller & Steve Heiman were focusing on logic and analysis to develop a "win-win" sales approach that is alive and well at the Miller-Heiman Corporation.

For decades salespeople had been trained to focus on demonstrating features and benefits - "educating their prospective customers". This developed into a consultative type solution sale, where sales people approached customers from a different perspective. They were taught to focus on finding their customers' "pains" and then tailoring their product or service to meet these needs and present this as the solution.

Moving forward, in 2002 Mike Schultz and John Doerr founded the RAIN Group with a research-based approach to selling based on in-depth customer feedback.

The next big disruption in sales methodology came in 2011 with the publication of The Challenger Sale by Matthew Dixon and Brent Adamson, who proposed that "solution selling" was dead and that disrupting the customers' buying process, uncovering unrecognised needs and then fulfilling them would lead to sales success.

The debate between these different methodologies continues to rage on. Whilst acknowledging that previous methods still have some valuable aspects, they are now no longer fully aligned with many of your customers' buying processes.

Unfortunately, many very successful sales people have seen their careers decline over the last few years as they have not been able or willing to adapt to this new sales reality.

The reality is Customers are in control, not sales people.

Today's customers have access to 90% of the information they need to make a purchasing decision. They come to the table armed to the teeth with analysis, peer reviews, competitor pricing models and all the social proof they need.
In many cases, they no longer want or need a sales person wasting time educating them on their products, services or the marketplace. They are already on it.

Similarly, customers are more advanced and adept at identifying their issues or challenges and often start the buying/sales process with a good idea of how to resolve them.

Hence, many of these older consultative solution-led sales approaches feel out of sync with a customer that is already quite far along in the buying process before they ever need to engage with you.

Often there is not a "pain" at all. They are not broken and don't need fixing! They are already very successful and their focus is on growth and achieving their future key objectives.

With all these changes in buying behavior, we might ask...

How can I stay relevant and valuable today in a customer's eyes?

>>>>>>>>>>

Salespeople need to acknowledge this change in the starting point.

Customers who previously were happy to engage in an in-depth conversation about their issues and then have you work up a solution are now expecting you to:

a) rapidly digest their situation and
b) quickly demonstrate you clearly understand their needs.

But this doesn't mean you'll win the sale this is now just the entry price to get you on the starting line!

CHAPTER 2.

What do today's customers really want from you?

It's vital that salespeople fully understand that customers are looking for different attributes from salespeople today than they were five years ago.

A very interesting survey conducted by the US-based RAIN Group identified some fundamental differences between high-achieving salespeople and those coming in second place.

TOP TEN QUALITIES CUSTOMERS VALUE MOST

1. Educated me with new ideas or perspectives.
2. Collaborated with me.
3. Persuaded me we would achieve new ideas or results.
4. Listened to me.
5. Understood, my needs.
6. Helped me avoid potential pitfalls.
7. Crafted a compelling solution.
8. Depicted purchasing process accurately.
9. Connected with me personally.
10. Overall value to the company is superior to other options.

It's interesting to note that of these top ten attributes only the last one involves the organisation, all the others focus on the individual.

This underlines the critical role the salesperson plays and how vital their performance is on who will win the sale.

So where are we heading next in the world of sales?

>>>>>>>>>

I really want to encourage you, as a sales leader or sales professional, to stop and take stock of where you are in your sales management and sales approach to clients. It's a great time for adaptation to the new sales environment. New technology is making highly mobile and fast CRM adoption a must. Together with new inbound marketing techniques, it's an exciting time for developing your sales approach. The need for individuals and companies to embrace these changes is paramount, as you want not just to survive but to **Thrive** in the new sales reality.

Why not take the following assessment to see how well you are adapting to the evolving sales environment.

ASSESSMENT 1.

Attributes of top performing sales people.

Take this short assessment to compare your sales approach with the qualities most valued by today's customer.

The score of "1" means you need serious work in this area and a score of "5" means you could give lessons to others in this area.

Be honest with yourself.

By educating yourself on the qualities clients most value, we can work to develop them further and increase our relevance to those clients.

1. How often are you creating and sharing new ideas, content and insights with clients?
1 – 2 – 3 – 4 – 5

2. Do your meeting preparation and research allow you to rapidly digest a client's situation and quickly demonstrate you clearly understand their needs?
1 – 2 – 3 – 4 – 5

3. Is your focus on finding client "pains" or on identifying areas to collaborate together to help them achieve their key objectives?
1 – 2 – 3 – 4 – 5

4. Is your approach aimed at challenging or disrupting their buying process? Or is your aim to connect with them personally, actively listening and demonstrating you have understood their needs?
1 – 2 – 3 – 4 – 5

5. Do you regularly help clients to identify and avoid potential pitfalls? Are you regularly educating them on the latest trends and industry changes affecting their business?
1 – 2 – 3 – 4 – 5

SCORES

Your Total Score is 0-5

You are probably comfortable using old approaches that have worked in the past. Seek out some sales training and current education to refresh your sales approach.

Suggested Action:

Consider both a coach for one-on-one development and formal sales training and education. If you are in a senior sales position, do not make the same mistake many professionals make—not keeping up to date. Ensure you get relevant training and education. Do not let your successful career decline. Secure your training and develop your career even further!

Your Total Score is 6-11

You are in need of some development (everyone has to learn and adapt to the specifics of the new sales reality).

Suggested Action:

Consider signing up for a sales training and education program that focuses on developing the key qualities valued by clients. Everyone learns how to improve their approach either through the hard knocks of experience or via training and education. The latter is more desirable than the former for a myriad of reasons.

Your Total Score is 12-17
You are average, and that is not acceptable.

Suggested Action:

Being average is not acceptable to any person and you have the potential to make rapid improvements. Consider one-on-one coaching or sign-up for a relevant sales training and education program.

Your Total Score is 18-25
You have an excellent sales approach; work on developing and refreshing your skills.

Suggested Action:

You are on the right path to becoming an outstanding sales professional and beyond. Consider engaging with a coach for focused sales development to reach your full potential.

CHAPTER 3.

The Sales Strategist gets started

With all this rapid change, where do you start to create a winning sales strategy?

Start at a place that will enable you to achieve all your business objectives.

A strong sales strategy is foundational to your success. Maybe you are looking for growth in new market sectors, increased revenue from existing accounts or introducing new products or services. Do you have the appropriate strategy? Reviewing and creating a solid sales strategy is the first step.

All too often a sales strategy is created without spending enough time consulting customers to ensure it supports their key business needs and objectives, and plays to your business strengths. So before starting the creation of your strategy, why not ask the folks you're writing the strategy for what they think?

You can gain incredible insight into how effective your sales proposition is by holding win / loss reviews with existing and prospective customers. You can set the expectation for this if you explain early in your initial meetings that, regardless of the outcome, you would really appreciate an opportunity to review briefly with them their buying process to assist you in making continual improvements to the service you provide them.

A CUSTOMER FOCUSED SALES STRATEGY

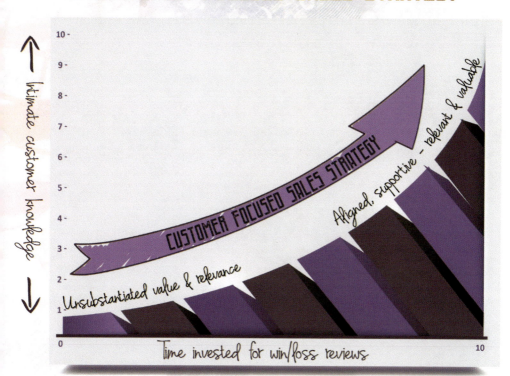

Y-axis: Intimate customer knowledge

Labels on chart: Unsubstantiated value & relevance; CUSTOMER FOCUSED SALES STRATEGY; Aligned, supportive - relevant & valuable

X-axis: Time invested for win/loss reviews

Most customers are happy to engage in this brief 30-40min review and you can gain some precious insights on where your customers found value and which areas of the sales / buying process from their point of view need improving. I've found this is one of the fastest ways to make rapid improvement in your understanding of client needs. This vital knowledge can then form part of the basis for a well-considered customer-focused sales strategy, one that does deliver results directly to your client's needs.

From a practical point of view, these reviews deliver the best and most objective feedback when they are conducted by either an external party or a colleague who has not been directly involved in the sales process.

I've seen companies frequently attempt to enter new markets with their same old strategy only to meet with failure. The strategy must be tailored to suit the market sector and add value to the customer.

Real life example. This point was demonstrated to me whilst working with a global ceiling and flooring manufacturer who decided to enter a new market sector. Their strategy was to focus on attracting business from architects and interior designers. Unfortunately, their knowledge of this customer type, their needs and challenges were limited. Additionally, they didn't appreciate fully how or where to influence this new type of customer. Ultimately, gaining traction in this new sector was slow. The approach that had been successful previously with main construction contractors didn't appeal to the needs and aspirations of the new prospective clients. This resulted in a whole range of specially designed and high margin products not achieving their full revenue potential for the company.

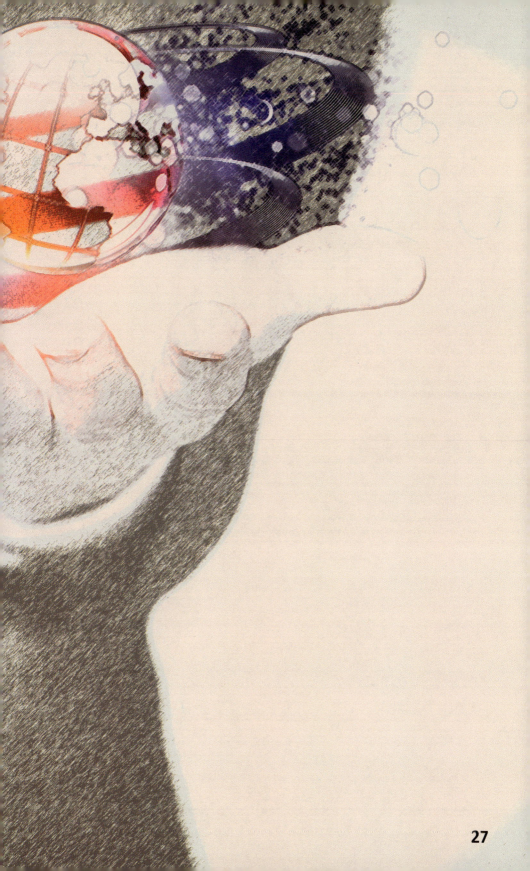

CHAPTER 4.

Why over complicated strategy sucks!

>>>>>>>>>

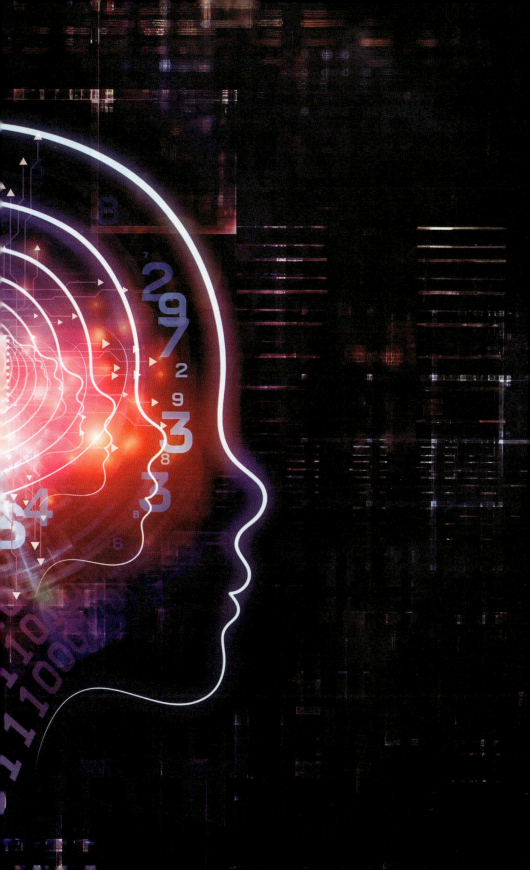

Many individuals go cold when they hear the word "strategy".

It's seen by many as an esoteric art practiced only by an enlightened few; those in the organisation deemed responsible for guiding the company to future growth and prosperity. I think this is a shame as many of these people have extensive experience and can provide valuable insights.

One reason for this lack of enthusiasm could be the approach many companies take each year in organising their strategy retreat. I've heard from many company executives about the days and weeks they expend in preparation for their PowerPoint presentations for the board.

Then on the given day everyone shows up, set the task of being creative and innovative for a few hours to enable a stellar strategy to be produced before COB.

When you consider the contrived nature and format of these strategy sessions, it's not surprising many companies find it is difficult to stimulate fresh thinking among their senior management.

Let's face it: When was the last time you had a brilliant idea? I'd like to bet it wasn't when you were obliged to sit in a room of your peers all day and told to brainstorm the next strategy.

You were probably out walking the dog or in the shower! Normally, these genius moments take place when you're doing something totally unrelated.

Frequently the upshot of all this time and effort is an overly complicated plan.

Once all the detailed analysis, "blue sky thinking" and future trending have been collated, along with the key business objectives, the business plan has morphed into a significant piece of literature worthy of a hardcover binding. Upon closer inspection, however, the strategy is often strikingly light on the specific actions needed to implement it successfully in the field.

The result?

A comprehensive document that often sits gathering dust until it's picked up just prior to the next annual review.

This is why your ability to create and communicate a pragmatic sales strategy is so, vital.

CHAPTER 5.

Let's create a transparent sales strategy that cuts to the chase!

>>>>>>>>>>

Creating your sales strategy should be an exciting and motivating exercise. But here's the challenge...ensuring you have clarity.

All too often the sales strategy is Opaque to the rest of the organisation. In fact, it's so poorly Communicated that when you ask the staff, they struggle to articulate it and, as a consequence, they can't see how <u>their daily actions</u> affect the achievement of key objectives.

Daily Tasks × Time = LONG TERM RESULTS

However, there is something far worse and that is a Translucent sales strategy, one where people "think" they understand what needs to be done, but it's not completely clear. This is dangerous as it causes **confusion** and **conflicting** approaches!

Only a Transparent strategy that is clearly communicated and fully understood is of true value.

Transparent

Transparent objects allow all of the light to pass through them. This means that we can clearly see through them.

Translucent

Translucent objects only allow some light to pass through them. This means that we can partially see through them.

Opaque

Opaque objects do not allow any light to pass though them. This means that we cannot see through them at all.

So, how do I create this type of transparent winning sales strategy?

The answer to creating a transparent and pragmatic sales strategy lies in clearly identifying the key sales objectives needed to achieve your business goal. Then reversing back and selecting the most effective sales activities to achieve these objectives.

35

Finally, pick some key metrics to measure the chosen activities so you can monitor your progress and keep on track. Practise using the technique in Diagram 3. to sharpen your skills.

You have now created within this one-page document a clear strategy to communicate with your team. This is not a dusty business plan but rather a live, working document that you can review frequently to monitor your progress and ensure you are on track to achieve your results throughout the year.

Having this clarity enables you to give your sales team clear direction on how to achieve their sales objectives. You can then manage the team by focusing on the right metrics and predictably link the business results desired in the boardroom with the sales activities on the ground.

Without this direct link, it's almost impossible to get clarity and control over the implementation of your sales strategy.

It will also stop your sales managers drowning in a sea of data, as it focuses their attention on the few metrics that really matter. Ultimately, you will be on the right track, creating a clear set of operating instructions to drive the sales team to consistently higher performance.

This clarity enables the sales department to join their peers in finance and production as a professional management discipline. Why not take this short assessment to compare your skill in setting a pragmatic sales strategy with top sales management practice?

ASSESSMENT FOR CREATING SALES STRATEGY

Take this short assessment to compare your skill in setting pragmatic sales strategy with top sales management practice.

Read through the five forecasting questions and give yourself an honest assessment from 1 to 5.

The score of "1" means you need serious work in the area and a score of "5" means you could give lessons to others in the area.

Be honest with yourself.

Creating a pragmatic sales strategy starts with a clear understanding of the link between the results reported in the boardroom and the sales activities in the field.

1.

Have you clearly identified where your growth revenue will come from? This could involve determining what percentage of sales will be contributed from the different market sectors. Or which products and services you will focus on to achieve the sales revenue growth desired? Is the growth from developing existing clients or finding new business?
1 – 2 – 3 – 4 – 5

2. ***Have you selected your top sales objectives to achieve this growth?*** You need to analyse the above answers and select the most appropriate objectives to achieve them. For example: You could set the objective of presenting the new product range to 15 key accounts in Q1. Or to increase showroom footfall by 25% this year.
1 – 2 – 3 – 4 – 5

3. ***Have you chosen the specific sales activities the sales team need to complete to achieve these objectives?*** You need to link the specific sales activites to the above objectives. For example: Organise five new product presentations with Key Accounts per month in Q1. Or each salesperson to organise two showroom visits per month throughout the year.
1 – 2 – 3 – 4 – 5

4. ***What level of visability and control do your sales metrics provide?*** To gain visibility and control over your results you need to select a few key metrics to measure these activities and ensure you are on track. For example: Number of Key Account presentations per month. Or Number of client showroom visits per month.
1 – 2 – 3 – 4 – 5

5. ***How well have you communicated your strategy to the sales team?*** You need to ensure you have communicated clearly the sales strategy to your sales team. Explain how their daily sales activities are inextricably linked to achieving the sales objectives and how their contribution greatly affects the overall company results to increase engagement.
1 – 2 – 3 – 4 – 5

SCORES

Your Total Score is 0-5

You are probably new to creating sales strategy seek out some sales management training and education.

Suggested Action:

Consider both a coach for one-on-one development and formal sales management training and education. If you are in your first sales management position, do not make the same mistake most new to management make—not getting any training and education. Most ascend to their first sales management position at the age of 32 years old.

The average age of a person getting their first sales management training or education is 42 years old. Do not let that be you; secure your training and develop your career!

Your Total Score is 6-11

You are in need of some development (everyone has to learn the specifics for setting strategy).

Suggested Action:

Consider signing up for a sales strategy training and education program. Everyone learns how to manage their sales team either through the hard knocks of experience or training and education. The latter is more desirable than the former for a myriad of reasons.

Your Total Score is 12-17
You are average, and that is not acceptable.

Suggested Action:

Being average is not acceptable to any person. Consider one-on-one coaching or sign-up for a sales strategy training and education program.

Your Total Score is 18-25
You are excellent at setting sales strategy; work on developing and refreshing your skills.

Suggested Action:

You are on the right path to becoming an outstanding sales manager and beyond. Consider engaging with a coach for focused sales management development to reach your full potential.

CHAPTER 6.

Recruiting an All-Star Sales Team.

What are the attributes of a great salesperson?

When you are creating a world-class sales team, there are so many factors demanding your attention: hiring, training, coaching, pipeline forecasting...the list is endless.

Where should you focus your precious time and energy?

>>>>>>>>>

Recruiting the right people.

Focus on developing a first-class sales recruitment process. The value of this cannot be underestimated as it forms the foundation of all your sales management activities. To neglect, this aspect would be akin to building a house on sand rather than bedrock.

Just think for a moment: if you were asked to make a decision on purchasing a piece of equipment costing over £100,000. How would you approach it? No doubt you would clarify exactly what features you needed: you would do extensive market research, review the alternatives, and evaluate the risks before purchasing. The irony is many managers spend a little over 2 x 60 mins with first and second interviews before hiring.

Many sales managers, despite doing a great job of training and coaching their team, often "wing it" when it comes to recruiting and interviewing.

It takes a significant investment of time and real effort to find great people. However, even if you are excellent at sales training, managing, and forecasting, it won't be enough to compensate for a team of mediocre salespeople. Unfortunately, many sales managers don't invest the time to create a clear process that will enable them to predictably identify top sales performers.

They inevitably devote hours and hours each day to fire-fighting sales issues, coaching underperforming salespeople and chasing their monthly and quarterly sales targets, rather than finding top performers who will be able to consistently bring in great business results year after year.
So how can you create this outstanding sales recruitment process?

Here's the problem: It's different for every company. Oh great! I can hear you say...

Well here's why, each salesperson has their own strong suit or key strength. Some are great at consultative selling with questions and active listening; others are great relationship builders and effortlessly create rapport and lasting friendships. Still others produce exceptionally high activity levels and are well suited to high transactional sales situations.

All are potentially great salespeople...in THEIR appropriate CONTEXT.

>>>>>>>>>>

What is your SALES CONTEXT?

Complex multi-stage sales cycle

Fast Moving high transaction levels (FMCG)

End-user technology solutions

Architectural specification sales

However, they may not have the skills to succeed in a different context. So basing your hiring decision solely on their past successful performance is not enough. You need to figure out what kind of salesperson would be ideal for your company. For example, I've recently done some training and coaching with a very successful salesperson who was struggling at his new company. His challenge was, he came from an FMCG (fast moving consumer goods) background where purchase decisions were made quickly. He was frustrated by the longer gestation period found in a more complex sales environment and shortly afterward left the company.

I heard another a classic example very recently, I was chatting with a senior sales executive of an international social media advertising agency. He was explaining how the new CEO had decided to hire a bunch of mature, high-achieving salespeople from Oracle. These heavy hitters were supposed to hit the ground running and deliver significant sales growth from new and existing clients. The result was near disaster, as these old pros were now attempting to move into a totally new context. It's still technology but...selling social media platforms, something many of them were unfamiliar with and hardly using themselves! Once again context was king. These individuals were struggling to gain credibility with new prospects and losing existing clients and a rapid change in sales strategy was taken before any further business was lost!

So here's the good news: Even though recruitment is unique for each company, the process to follow applies to every company.

CHAPTER 7.

So what does your ideal salesperson really look like?

A vital first step in the recruitment process is to get clarity regarding the qualities you require from your sales person.

1. Create a list of ideal sales qualities.

• What qualities equal sales success at your company? Write a clear definition for each of these qualities so you can score potential candidates on a scale of 1-10.

Key Criteria	Score	Weight	Weighted Score	Max Score
Coachabillity	8	9	72	90
Inquisitiveness	9	9	81	90
Dillgence	7	8	56	80
Proactivity	6	8	48	80
Brand Appearance	4	7	28	70
Previous Achievement	8	5	40	50
Preparation	8	3	24	30
Adaptabillty Change	7	3	21	30
Competiveness	8	3	24	30
Brevity	6	3	18	30
Total			**412**	**580** 71%

2. Work out how to evaluate individuals for each quality.

- What questions could you ask to determine their behaviours?
- What pre-interview exercises could they complete?
- What role-plays would reveal these qualities?

3. Create a score card for the ideal sales qualities.

After each interview score the candidates out of 10 for each key quality (see above table). In this way, objective comparisons can be made of the various candidates.

If several members of staff are involved in the hiring process, then comparing scores can be really helpful in delivering additional perspectives. Especially when colleagues' opinions may be emotive or easily influenced by others, this approach gives some objectivity.

Moving forward, there is real value in collating all this information from the score cards.
In a few months' time, you will be in an optimal position to review progress. Some salespeople will be producing excellent results, whilst others may be progressing more slowly. However, you can learn from this and refine your selection criteria of key qualities to further improve the process.

What key qualities do the top performers have in common? — Add more weight to finding these.

Which qualities don't seem to have a major impact on success? — Downgrade these in importance.
What qualities are we missing? — Are there other areas or qualities we do need but are not searching for?

Now you have a process for recruiting that gives you more control and enables objective results rather than subjective "gut feel" when making these vital sales hiring decisions.

CHAPTER 8.

5 Winning Sales Attributes

and How to Identify them at Interview Stage

So what could be your key qualities?
I said earlier that every company
is different; however here are some
suggestions on the qualities that I've
found to be well worth considering.

In recent years the sales environment has changed dramatically. Customers now have true buying power. Prices, distribution, technical information is all in the public domain. In addition to the abundance of comparative sales, information is another factor: The lens of social media. Today every company and individual can be held accountable and reviewed publically!

In this new sales forum the qualities formally associated with top performing salespeople - the aggressive, strong closers and objection handlers - now seem like dinosaurs from a bygone sales era.
Today's customers no longer accept high-pressure sales tactics. However, they do respond to respectful, helpful and smart salespeople who understand their needs.

What qualities do you need to look for? And how can you identify them at the interview stage? Here are my top five:

1. COACHABILITY

This is the ability to be reflective, allowing them to absorb coaching and to be able to effectively apply it for improvement.

During the interview, set up a small role play that mirrors your own sales environment. For example, ask them to do a follow-up call on a sales lead; their goal is to do some basic discovery and set up an appointment to discuss the prospect's needs further.

After the exercise, ask them: "How do you think you did?" – Their response is your first insight as to how coachable they are. Do they reflect or analyse their performance?
I'm looking for specific points they felt they did well and what areas they could have improved. Someone who is highly coachable will be able to reflect, self-diagnose and propose improvements to weak areas.

The next step is to see their ability to absorb and apply coaching. Some people struggle to absorb coaching either because they are poor listeners or maybe they don't see the value of constructive feedback. Others absorb it but struggle to apply it; maybe they are less adaptable to change or improvement. You want to hire people who can both absorb and apply coaching.

Offer them one piece of positive feedback and one area of improvement. Coach them in this area, just a couple of points that your company has found successful. Ask them to do the role play again but this time incorporate the new ideas. Don't expect them to be perfect at it. What you are looking for is their real effort to apply what they have just been shown and their attitude to making improvement via coaching.

2. INQUISITIVENESS

Genuine personal interest in customers. The ability to understand their situation and challenges via effective questioning and active listening.

From the moment you meet them in reception, do they start by asking you questions, about your day, or reference a point from their research on the website? Do they follow up on my answers with thoughtful, intelligent, open-ended questions to learn more? If so this is a good start to the interview.

During the interview, do they ask meaningful questions? Are they curious to understand our current situation, our goals, and challenges? Does their train of thought reflect that they have actually listened carefully to your responses? Do they ask questions to confirm back that they have understood you correctly?

Also during the second attempt at the role play do they display a good level of questioning and listening to gain a deeper level of understanding regarding your needs?

3. DILIGENCE

Their level of care and attentiveness in meeting preparation, sales reporting, and opportunity tracking. Their dedication to the completion of sales tasks.

Does this individual have the self-discipline required to proactively communicate with customers throughout the sales process? Are they truly customer focused?
How do they feel about using and keeping a CRM system up to date?

Do their answers suggest they consider it a necessary evil? Or as a key tool to allow them to be effective and efficient.

Pose a customer scenario involving a complaint or service level issue. Ask them for two or three alternative ways of resolving it and which one they would recommend?
What do they think are the most important metrics to measure sales performance?

How do they manage and track their sales opportunities from lead to order?

4. PROACTIVITY

An inner drive and sense of daily urgency to pursue the company mission with real energy.

This drive seems to be an innate quality of top performers. They need and value themselves based on achieving results.

Ask them, if they started tomorrow how would they set their sales priorities?

What would their typical day, week or month look like? How would that be organised?

Do their answers show a structured way of working? Is it one that focuses on achieving predetermined key sales objectives or alternatively do they focus on whatever is the most compelling and urgent issue that day?

How would they plan to achieve their annual sales target?

Look to see if they are aware of the key sales processes.
For example:
Would they engage in Territory Management to qualify their most valuable customers? Would they identify A, B & C status to plan their call frequency proportionately.

Do they mention Account Management for larger key clients, the creation of organisational charts for each one to highlight the key individuals they would target, to protect and develop the account revenue?

What sales activities and events have they found to be most effective?

I'm looking for some strategy and preparation versus a "fly by the seat of my pants" mind-set. Do they plan ahead and create a 12 - month Activity Plan with slots and dates booked for key activities and events with prospects and key clients.

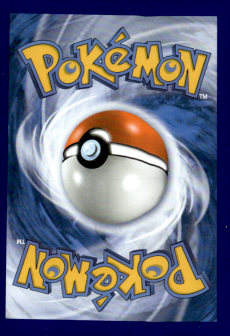

TRAINER

Supporter

Hau

Draw 3 cards.

You may play only 1 Supporter card during your turn *(before your attack)*.

Illus. Ken Sugimori   61/73 ◇
©2017 Pokémon

5. THEIR PREVIOUS ACHIEVEMENT

Do they have a track-record of high achievement and top performance in their lives? E.g. Career, Academic, Sporting, Military, Sales etc.

This is relatively easy to evaluate if they come from a medium to large sales force (50-100 salespeople). You can ask about where they ranked, what metrics were used for the ranking, their overall results against the target for the last three years etc.

It's more challenging if they come from a smaller organisation or if they don't have a sales background at all. In this case, I'd look for excellent performance in other areas of their lives. What examination results did they achieve? Were they involved in captaining a sports team to a championship win? Were they involved in leading an extracurricular organisation? Basically, what separated them in terms of achievement from their peers?

Individuals who have performed at the top percentile level are likely to bring that same drive, competitiveness and passion to their sales role.

So select the key qualities that make people successful in your company. Create and implement a first-class sales recruitment process and you will be well on your way to hiring the right people to rapidly grow your business.

CHAPTER 9.

Creating a Well-Oiled Machine-

The process that moves the group in unison

Is Sales Really a Professional Management Discipline?

Most companies allocate a budget for training their front line salespeople. The common logic is that as these people are face-to-face with clients, they hold the key to sales performance.

Their skill level is undoubtedly a key factor in a company's success. However, an often greater influence on results is being overlooked: that of the sales director or manager.

In a significant number of firms, there is a lack of investment at the sales management level. Often this is due to the assumption that a great salesperson will naturally evolve into a great manager. But sales and sales management are two very different skill sets.

So what should you study to become a great sales manager?

Herein lies a fundamental problem. We are missing the operating instructions for a sales team.

Other departments in the company are much more advanced than sales in this aspect. They enjoy a fundamental understanding of their internal workings and are able to direct their day-to-day business with confidence toward their ultimate objectives.

Finance, for example, involves a strong set of metrics with clearly understood implications. Any finance professional can easily analyse and discuss the relationships between income statements, balance sheets, and cash flow. It's a common language; they have a discipline.

Manufacturing too has a set of recognised processes to control and direct production. Ask any plant manager and he can give you a list of standard measures such as throughput, defects, and quality control with a clear understanding of how one impacts the other to guide higher performance.

Sales have somehow evaded the management structure and professional discipline of its peer groups. There is no sales equivalent of GAAP or ISO standards.

Compared to finance and manufacturing, the discipline of sales is still in its infancy.

When information technology came along, sales had no formal operating instructions for itself. So sales CRM systems were layered on top of unstructured processes and inconsistent execution.

Simply put, sales automated its own form of chaos.

In today's complex selling environment you need a structured process to help you manage effectively. However, it's no good simply rolling out sales processes across the entire sales force, in cookie-cutter fashion. They won't be efficient or productive and will most likely lead to resistance from your team. You need to understand how the different sales management processes work and who in the organisation should be using them and when.

Here's an example. Recently, I was asked by a managing director: "So what's the best sales process for our company?"

My answer, " Well Jeff, it's specific to each company", was met with a groan, as you can imagine. However, I went on to explain it was just his question that was wrong. You see previously, he had been trying to apply sales processes wholesale across the company, regardless of the individual sales roles and responsibilities. He was requesting reports that were relevant to certain salespeople but irrelevant to others. As you can imagine his team wasn't overly enamoured by this approach.

A better question to ask is, "What sales process adds value to this particular role?"

You see, the sales management process you apply is solely based upon the individual sales role.

Do you have specific sales processes in place based upon the individual sales roles in your company?
For example, if your salespeople are covering a geographic area or territory with multiple customers, are you providing guidance on effective Territory Management and Call Frequency?

On the other hand, what if you were selecting a sales process to effectively manage a key account salesperson? Would you still need to use Territory Management? Probably not.

They already know who their top key clients are, so of more value would be to have some great Account Management in place to protect and develop future revenue.

So you get the picture: The sales process will be unique for each company, however, the methodology for creating the sales process is consistent.

First, identify the specific sales roles in your company and then only select the sales management processes that maximise the efficiency and productivity of that specific sales role.

So let's see how we can take a big stride forward in establishing a rigorous sales management discipline using five key sales processes.

THE RIGHT SALES PROCESS FOR THE SALES ROLE

	Sales roles		
	Territory sales Representative	National Account Manager	Inside Sales Representative
Call Management	☑	☑	
Opportunity Management			
Account Management		☑	
Territory Management	☑		☑
Sales Force Enablement			

↑ Sales processes ↓

CHAPTER 10.

The Five Pillars of Sales Management

>>>>>>>>

To transform sales chaos into a professional management discipline, here are the five pillars of sales management.

However, don't make the classic mistake of imposing formal processes across the entire sales force. As you will see from the diagram below too little process and it won't be effective; too much and you will meet resistance and no adoption from your team.

RIGHTSIZING YOUR SALES PROCESS

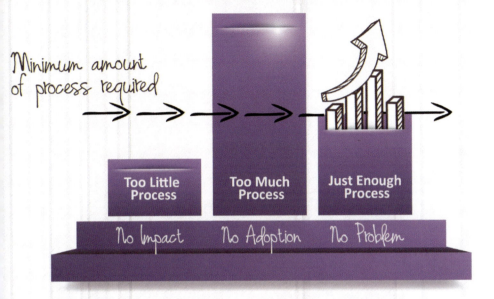

Minimum amount of process required

Too Little Process

Too Much Process

Just Enough Process

No Impact

No Adoption

No Problem

Choosing the Right Sales Process is Dependent on the Individual Selling Roles.

- Territory Management -
  Allocating effort efficiently across different types of customers.
- Account Management -
  Maximising long-term value from a single customer.
- Opportunity Management -
  Strategically navigating a multi-call sales cycle.
- Call Management -
  Planning & conducting individual customer interactions.
- Sales Team Empowerment -
  Development of the skills in these four areas.

Using these five processes, you can create a perfectly aligned sales management model for your company.

Let's unpack these processes a little more so you can see how they can be applied effectively:

>>>>>>>>>>

TERRITORY MANAGEMENT

Too often a salesperson will be given their territory with little guidance on how to maximise their efforts, and it's the sales manager's responsibility to provide this clear direction.

If the company CRM has been kept up to date you should easily be able to determine who are the key clients. Pareto's old 80/20 principle is a useful guide as it will highlight which are the 20% of customers that generally are responsible for 80% of revenue.

Classify each account and give them a status level, for example, A, B or C.

It's amazing to me the number of times I've done this exercise with literally hundreds of salespeople. We start by identifying the total number of accounts they have; this can vary but often it's 300-400. I've even sat down with a young saleswoman who proudly stated she had 1000!

But here is the point: What frequency do you need to call on them to achieve the maximum level of sales?
You only have a finite amount of selling days per year. As you will see in the example below it's probably somewhere around 200.

So how many accounts should you be trying to develop? That will vary depending on how frequently you need to see them. But let's say for argument's sake you will visit your A Accounts once a month. You will plan to visit all of your B Accounts once a quarter. Your C Accounts you will target via email marketing every quarter.

You also need to allow time to follow up on requests from your customer meetings, quotations, and time to track your sales opportunities. Plus you will need some time to respond to inbound sales leads and enquiries.

As you can see from the Call Frequency example below this salesperson can only effectively manage 65 accounts in total.

That may not sound like very many, but experience has shown me that once the number of accounts starts to climb there is a corresponding drop in the depth of relationship with each customer. Also, the quality of the follow-up work in tracking good sales opportunities falls significantly, leading to a lower sales conversion rate...and then you're into the "busy fool" syndrome.

Territory & Call Frequency Management example.

- 52 Weeks – minus - 4 weeks holiday
- 48 Weeks - minus - 2 weeks sickness
- 46 Weeks - 2 weeks (Sales Meetings/Exhibitions/ Internal meetings/Training)
- 44 Weeks x 5 = 220 days.
- Based on 220 working days a year = potentially 704 meetings / visits per year.
- That is based on 16 meetings per week, averaging 3.2 per day.
- **15 Status A accounts** called on monthly which totals 180 calls,
- **50 Status B accounts** called on quarterly which totals 200 calls.
- This leaves 324 available calls for new enquiries, tracking sales opportunities & new potential accounts.
- **Getting this balance is essential to managing your time effectively, achieving top productivity and delivering superb customer responsiveness.**

ACCOUNT MANAGEMENT

Most account management plans are useless. Here are four reasons why they don't work.

1. Most are created in January, reviewed annually and quickly gather dust.

2. There's no client input.

3. There are no mutually agreed goals.

4. They don't proactively add more value to the client.

Developing effective Account Management plans is a vital activity. There are two key goals to focus on: The first is to **protect** your account from competition. The second is to proactively **develop** and grow the business from this valuable customer.

Here are four keys to include in your planning strategy.

1. Invite the active participation of your clients to co-create the plan with you.

2. Identify your clients' key objectives and agree how you can best support them in achieving these goals..

3. Review the plans every 90 days; they should have objectives, activities, and metrics to see if you are both achieving your goals.

4. Continually impart value both in small and big deeds throughout the year.
For example:

a. Are you publishing a special report with content they would benefit from?

b. Could you introduce them to an industry expert and share their valuable experience?

c. Could you provide the latest sector-specific news and show the potential effects to their business?

d. Finally, share some relevant case studies with them on how your best clients have succeeded in overcoming current challenges.

4 KEYS TO INCREASING CUSTOMER LOYALTY & REVENUE

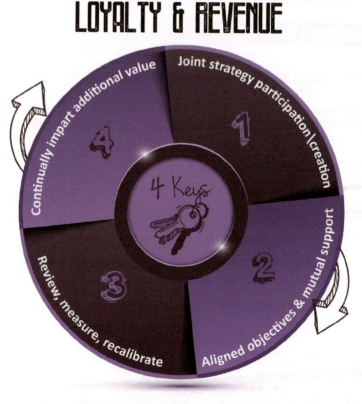

OPPORTUNITY MANAGEMENT

This is one of my favourite sales activities because it will:

Help you to win more sales with less effort.

It enables salespeople to spend their time wisely, by only working on realistic and achievable sales opportunities. It's about achieving more in less time and with a lot less stress! I liken it to the difference between a scatter gun approach – commonly known as "throwing mud against the wall, hoping some will stick" versus the alternative - a professional sniper's approach. They have done their preparation, and they're cool, calm, confident and completely focused on hitting their target.

In essence, there are five key areas you must cover on any sales opportunity, and these are the winning elements.

Have you ever wondered why you win or lose a sale?

Your understanding of these key areas will reveal the reasons behind why you win or lose a deal. By endeavouring to gain an in-depth understanding of these elements, you will allow yourself the opportunity to increase your sales conversion rates rapidly.

Which means you won't have to work as hard to achieve the same results.

In the next chapter, we will discuss why opportunity management is where a sales manager should spend his time and energy to maximise the team's development.

THE 5 WINNING ELEMENTS

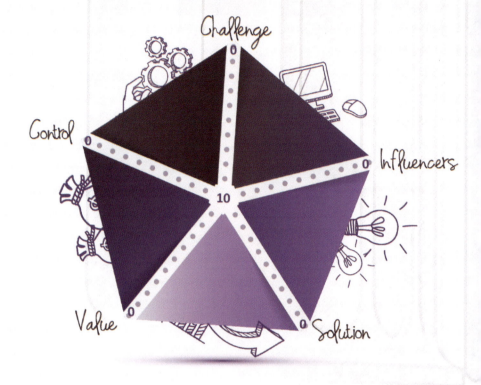

5 key questions to deal with

- **Challenge:** Is the project likely to happen now?
- **Influencers:** Are we aligned with all the people that influence the decision?
- **Solution:** Does the buyer really prefer our solution?
- **Value:** Does the project provide mutual value?
- **Control:** Do we have full control over the buyer's decision-making process?

CALL MANAGEMENT

You have successfully achieved an appointment to see a new client. Your preparation is key, too many sales people roll up to customer meetings without doing their homework.

So prepare relentlessly, do some in-depth web research on the customer. What are the trends in their industry sector? Ensure you know of any previous connection to your company. Don't rely on your CRM, seek out any colleagues who may have serviced the account before. Frequently, people have this information in their heads but it's never made it into the CRM customer data. This kind of preparation invariably pays big dividends in allowing you to rapidly understand a potential client's situation.

Now you need to consider the following:

- Why are you going to see the client?
- What do you intend to achieve?
- How can you make the most of that first meeting?
- What do you want the outcome to be?

Frequently, businesspeople fail to set a clear objective or even think about the outcome that they want from the meeting. Most people think they have set an objective by stating that they wish to "build the relationship" or "just gather information".
But these objectives are too vague and woolly. Set a smarter goal.

Here's a quick reminder of the old SMART rules on how to create a clear objective.

- **S** Specific
- **M** Measurable
- **A** Actionable
- **R** Realistic
- **T** It has a timescale

In a nutshell, your objective must always be to **"gain a commitment to the next step"**.

So before every meeting take the time to get your head in the game, write out your P-C-P. It will keep you on track, focused on your objective and allow both you and your customer to get the maximum benefit from your valuable time together.

3 KEYS TO PRODUCTIVE MEETINGS

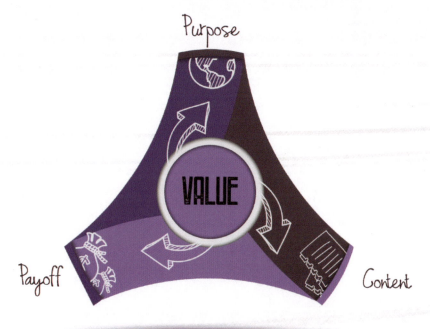

- *Purpose*
  Why am I having this meeting?
- *Content*
  What points do I need to cover?
- *Payoff*
  What is my next objective?

SALES TEAM EMPOWERMENT

This fifth pillar is the ongoing consistent commitment to the development of your sales team.

No-one can stand still or should want to; we all need to grow and develop our skills and abilities. Sales results are always built on the sound execution of the right sales activities. As a sales leader, it's your responsibility to realise that all of these activities are executed by individuals and their capability plays a significant role in the effectiveness of their execution.

Developing high-quality salespeople is key to sustainable growth year in year out. Investing heavily in developing their sales force is a key strategy for many top companies. They see this Sales Team Empowerment as an investment that pays huge dividends, as the improved execution of activities delivers significant results.

CHAPTER 11.

Attributes of a Great Sales Leader

>>>>>>>>>

In addition to all the strategies and tactics of sales management we've just discussed, there's another aspect to your success which is much more closely related to your own personal development.

It's your ability to communicate and positively influence your team.

What's really interesting is that your success in this area is based almost entirely on just two key factors:

- Your Character:
The personal qualities you need to develop to lead with authenticity...and
- Your Skills:
The current and relevant skills required to perform at the top of your game.

You really need this holistic approach to provide you with both the personal and professional development required for long-term, sustainable success.

It's probably true that everyone would like to be a better leader and be able to positively influence others.

I'm going to use leadership and influence synonymously here because, when you really get down to its core, leadership is really the ability to communicate and influence people so that they listen and are moved to act, to change their thoughts or behaviour.

So if this is not happening, then really you are not influencing them or leading them.

Now you might not necessarily think of yourself as a leader. Often people are promoted to positions of responsibility based on their previous personal success, rather than their ability to lead others. A situation that is all too frequent in sales, is when top performers are seen as the next potential top managers. Unfortunately, the two roles are very different and require completely different skill sets!

The reality is that in every area of life we are called to lead. Whether that is in sales, as a parent, a school football coach or as a company MD. We are all leading and influencing others. So it makes sense to invest the time to understand how you can become exemplary in this area.

The world is crying out for men and women who can get things done; in every company, there is a constant need for true leaders. But what allows these individuals to have so much impact?

Here is a small exercise which I'd like to invite you to do:

List below two or three people you consider to be great leaders? (They can be from history or alive today.)

_____

_____

_____

_____

Next, list what you think are the top ten characteristics of great leaders.

_____   _____

_____   _____

_____   _____

_____   _____

_____   _____

Now, as you look back at your list, ask yourself on each one.

Is this a character trait? Or is it a skill?

Does it have to do with who they are as a person?   Or is it a skill they have.

I've done this exercise many times with groups and individuals over the years and the result rarely changes. Nearly 100% of the time it's the character traits people choose rather than skills when they are describing great leaders.

That's because there is a core principle at play here;

*People decide, either consciously or subconsciously, whether they will **allow you** to influence them based on two fundamental factors: Your **Character** and your **Skills**.*

This means they will judge you based on who you are as a person plus how they perceive your skill level – what you do and how well you do it.

Based on these two factors they decide almost exclusively whether to follow you or not.

Can I ask you when was the last time your company sent you to a *4-hour character development program?*

Never, right? We tend to focus on developing skills and we need to; it is an important factor. However, when it comes to leading others, people are deciding first. Are we good people?

Did you notice that they **allow you** to lead or influence them? This ability to lead **is a gift** that they give you. It's their personal choice and they can take it away too at any time.

So, based on these principles, the only way to enhance your depth of influence is to improve your character and the skills you demonstrate day to day.

Now, you might not think of yourself as a leader and you may not be a good one, or at least not yet at your full potential. But with this understanding, you can now look to purposely develop the traits and skills of a great leader!

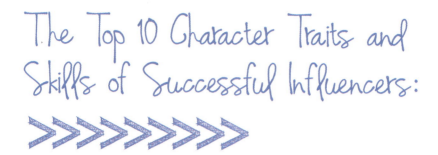

The Top 10 Character Traits and Skills of Successful Influencers:

>>>>>>>>>>

There are many fine personality traits that universally we value in others but especially in our leaders.

Here are some that have a positive influence on others. Developing yourself in these areas will enable you to become a better leader, influence more people, and make more sales, all from the right foundation.

You can own each of these; they are under your control. That is an important distinction to make, as there are some things you can't own or directly influence. Success comes when we learn how to own what is ours, do the best we can with it, and leave the rest alone.

1. SINCERITY

This quality is foundational to the ability to lead people. In essence, it is the genuineness of your motives, actions, and behaviour. It involves living your life in a way that is whole and undivided. The minute people see you are divided or have two codes of conduct, either in your personal or professional life, you break the trust and belief in you.

You are governed by your values and principles regardless of what may seem to be expedient or convenient circumstances of the moment.

2. COMMITMENT

Anyone that you seek to lead is bound to ask one question. How committed is the person asking me to be committed? You can't expect commitment from others if it's not clearly evident in you.

Is your commitment is demonstrated in these three areas of your life....

> **a.** Your Performance.
> Let me ask you when was the last time you met an athlete or a top business person that wasn't fully committed to it? It just doesn't happen, does it?
>
> Does your performance reflect your commitment to achieving top results?
>
> **b.** Your life's ambitions and victories.
> Looking longer-term do you demonstrate a commitment to achieving your goals.
>
> **c.** Your commitment affects your quality of life.

When was the last time you found somebody who was totally uncommitted with a very high quality of life?

It just doesn't happen.

So, are you committed to continually learning, growing and improving the quality of your life?

"The quality of a person's life is in direct proportion to their commitment to excellence, regardless of their chosen field of endeavour." Vince Lombardi.

3. ATTITUDE

How do others perceive your attitude? Is it positive or negative?

- Would your team describe you as an optimistic person?
- The root of the word "optimistic" is the word opt or to choose.
- You choose your Attitude.
- Who wants to follow a pessimist?
- Optimists lead people because people want to improve.

Fundamentally, you choose how you will see things.

This is done in a very specific way. Firstly, you need to understand the relationship between your thoughts, feelings, actions, and results.

You must be very aware of the thoughts you allow into your mind and control any negativity.

Your thoughts are powerful things and they directly control your emotions and feelings. These emotions will drive your beliefs, behaviour and actions, which ultimately create your results.

It takes real self-control to control your mind and its dominating thoughts but this is the only way to maintain a positive attitude, one that is not affected by circumstance.

"There is little difference in people, but that little difference makes a big difference. That little difference is attitude. The big difference is whether it is positive or negative."

- W. Clement Stone.

4. DECISIVENESS OR DECISION-MAKING

People want leaders to be decisive for two reasons:

a. Firstly, it breeds confidence in others. So if you don't make hard decisions they will lack trust in you.
If people become fearful, then they won't allow you to lead them.

b. Secondly, there is a pragmatic reason; people don't want to be kept waiting. For example, if you have to make a decision within the next 30 days you don't want to decide on Day 1 before you have all the information or have taken sufficient time to reflect. Likewise, you don't want to wait until Day 28 before deciding. Procrastination is not being decisive. However, there is another benefit of making decisions in a timely manner, and that is the potential option to change or adjust your decision if you feel it was wrong.

So, do good leaders make mistakes? Yes, they do, but they make timely decisions so if possible they will have time to change if it's a wrong move.

"In any moment of decision the best thing you can do is the right thing, the second best thing is the wrong thing, and the worst thing you can do is nothing." Theodore Roosevelt.

So, what decisions do you need to make? Are people waiting for you and thinking…"When is he or she going to make that decision?!"

>>>>>>>>>

5. EMPATHY

This is the ability to share someone else's feelings or experiences by imagining what it would be like to be in that person's situation. Developing this quality gives you insight and allows you to develop strong relationships with people as they see you have genuine personal interest in them.

6. DILIGENCE

Is there a high level of care and attentiveness in your work?

Is diligence evident in your preparation for meetings, sales reporting, and opportunity tracking?

Are you dedicated to the completion of any task you undertake?
This quality makes you reliable and breeds confidence in others.

7. ENTHUSIASM

People want to follow someone who is enthusiastic. It's an infectious quality affecting everyone around you.

So, are you motivated and proactive? Is there an inner drive and sense of daily urgency to pursue the company goal with real energy? This drive seems to be an innate quality of top leaders.

The three best ways to stay enthusiastic and motivated are:

a. To do it daily. Be committed to getting motivated. Just like you take a shower and get dressed every day, you just do it.

b. Find a reason, a motive to act, this will put a spring in your step and get you out the door every day.

c. Fuel your passion, invest in yourself, read, study your craft and develop your skills and abilities.

8. PRIORITIES

It isn't doing things right; it is doing the right things. Good is the enemy of the Best.

Today we have too many options, and each day we are confronted with new opportunities that could distract us from our focus.

Thus, setting priorities is a key leadership skill.

The most powerful word in the human language now is...No! You need to know what you want, and know what you don't want, as that is the secret to setting priorities, or setting sales strategy, or objectives, or daily activities. Once you decide, then do it.

9. HUMILITY

This quality allows you to have a balanced and modest view of your own abilities and importance.

It helps you to show real respect for others, their ideas, feelings, and experiences. Humour is a wonderful asset aligned with humility. The ability to laugh at yourself is indispensable in earning respect and loyalty from others.

10. RELATIONSHIPS

It is always about the relationship.
Even in the largest global deals, you are in fact dealing not with a multi-national but with one or a handful of key individuals, all of whom have chosen to have this relationship with you.

Here are six keys to creating influential relationships:

1. Your own integrity.
2. Spend time together.
3. Communicate openly & candidly.
4. You have to care about the other person.
5. Share bonding opportunities involving a real purpose.
6. Have a mutual investment in each other.

"The most important ingredient we put into any relationship is not what we say or do, but what we are. And if our words and our actions come from superficial human relations techniques (the personality ethic) rather than from our own inner core (the Character ethic), others will sense that duplicity. We simply won't be able to create and sustain the foundation necessary for effective interdependence."
- Stephen R. Covey

EXERCISE FOR IMPLEMENTATION

Write one thing you will DO, not just a warm fuzzy thought but actually, choose a quality to work on in the next week.

Apply these qualities and root them into your life. By improving your character and taking your skills to the next level, you will see people willingly listen to you and give you the gift of influence.

CHAPTER 12.

What are the Secrets to Maximizing your Team's Potential?

Visiting activity of the Web-site by hours

Worldwide customers a

Web-site traffic

Business activity of company and subdivisions

Relative activity of subdivisions of main company

Are you a Collaborative coach or a Cross-examining lawyer?

>>>>>>>>>>

What is your most important task as a sales leader?

Ultimately, it's to develop and maximise the potential of your sales team.

To achieve this, you need to multiply your effectiveness and transfer your experience, knowledge, and skills to your team.

This is not without its challenges. You can't be there to coach and assist at every meeting or every opportunity.

How can you influence your team without being physically present?

How can you get engagement and accountability from them?

The answers lie in a fundamental shift from traditional sales management practice to a more productive approach – focused on working collaboratively with your team to maximise results.

So, what's the difference?

Well, traditionally, for a sales manager to get a real grip on where sales opportunities are in the pipeline, he would have to sit down with his salesperson and inevitably start asking a lot of searching questions to see exactly how realistic their forecasted sales are.

This approach results in a virtual cross-examination. If the salesperson is vague in any area of information, the more the manager feels the need to push back with additional questions to clarify the situation. This only creates more tension as the salesperson will either defend their position, tell him what they think he wants to hear or simply end up justifying the situation and their existence.

So much time is wasted on these types of conversation, going over all the salesperson's situational knowledge, rather than focusing on the key information required to win the order. In addition to the wasted time, many managers find gaining agreement to the next specific actions required and future accountability frustratingly difficult to achieve.

However, this need not be the case, by creating a Collaborative Coaching environment. A sales manager can gain engagement from their people, add real value to the sales process, and get that elusive accountability they seek.

How is this achieved?

Use Smart Tools.

By using some simple but highly effective tools, managers can review potential sales opportunities together with their salespeople. Working together, they can see what information they currently know and what pieces of information are missing from the Compass Card TM – (a Gap analysis tool). The questions included in this tool are designed to focus the salesperson on the key winning elements in any deal. They are also the same questions an experienced manager would ask if he were in a meeting himself with the potential client.
The second component of the Compass Card is the "Win Plan" TM.

Once the gaps have been identified, the "Win Plan" is used to list all the specific actions the sales person needs to take in the coming days and weeks to close this opportunity.

Along with the specific action points, the salesperson is also asked to fill in any other resources or departments that are required to complete the action (i.e. input from the marketing department to create a proposal document). The initials of the person responsible for the action are noted along with the date for the action to be completed. The completed Compass Card and Win Plan are attached to the sales opportunity in the CRM as a record of the agreed next steps.

This has several major benefits:

>>>>>>>>>

1. A TRUSTING ATMOSPHERE

It allows a positive trusting atmosphere to develop between the manager and salesperson. It becomes a team effort as they review sales opportunities together side by side as they complete the Compass Card. The sales manager can add value in various ways, either from his previous experience in dealing with a similar situation or perhaps facilitating an introduction to someone he knows that could help his salesperson gain the needed information or influence they require.

2. POWERFUL KNOWLEDGE TRANSFER

Simultaneously, almost as if by a process of osmosis the salesperson is absorbing the knowledge and experience of their manager. They start to understand the value of the key questions and information needed to be successful in winning the opportunity. As the key information and questions asked rarely change, over the coming weeks and months the sales person starts adopting them as part of **their own** habitual questions when meeting with clients.

At this point both the manager and the salesperson are working off the same page, each one having a strong understanding of the key elements they need to cover in order to win. In this way, the manager is able to raise the standard and quality of his team's work.

Salespeople working at this higher level have a sense of pride in generating solid sales pipelines and accurate forecasts for their managers, which in turn creates a top- performance sales culture.

3. CREATES VOLITION & ACCOUNTABILITY

Using the Compass Card and Win Plan, a sales manager is able to add real value to his team. His salespeople benefit by receiving specific practical advice during these meetings and leave with a clear action plan to execute, moving them forward to win their key sales opportunities.

For the sales manager, he has finally achieved the goal of having clear accountability based on the specific actions they both agreed in the Win Plan, which he can quickly refer to at the next meeting saving him valuable time.

Additionally, by using these tools regularly on the 'must win' sales opportunities the sales manager can quickly and easily start to identify the particular areas where additional training or development are required to significantly increase an individual's performance.

By consistently applying these points you can create a positive coaching environment that encourages peak performance from each member of the team.

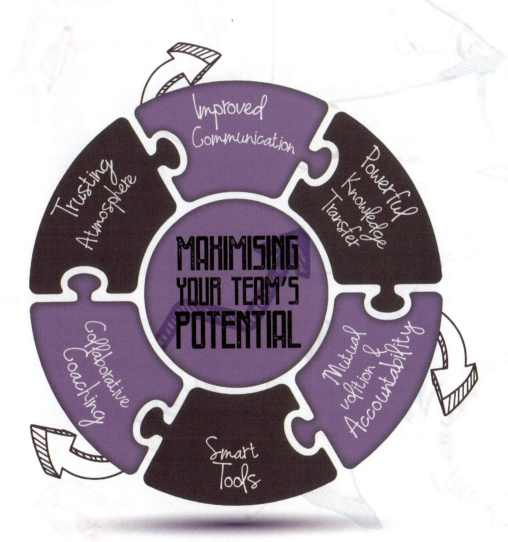

CHAPTER 13.

Creating the environment
for a high-performance sales
culture to flourish!

There are three key factors that overlap in creating the atmosphere for a high-performance sales culture to grow successfully.

>>>>>>>>

The 3 Factors for
CREATING A HIGH-PERFORMANCE SALES CULTURE

Earlier in this book we discussed in detail the importance of getting the right people onboard and in the right roles. We have also outlined the vital importance of the right sales process.

So, what is PLACE?

In the past, companies had differing opinions of the importance and value in their workplace. Often good design was seen as simply nice to have, and was quickly forsaken when budgets were reviewed. However, as younger generations of workers have joined the workforce even the staidest companies have had to rethink how they use their space.

In today's competitive marketplace, providing a great office space with informal breakout lounges, staff restaurants, and quiet zones for working away from open plan areas are becoming essential. Companies like Tesco, for example who previously had fairly standard offices, have recently invested in providing improved environments in order to attract good candidates and they are no alone as more and more traditional companies have seen the need to change.

Providing the right physical environment plays a significant role in productivity, staff retention and motivation.

The best sales environment should have a "buzz" and an energy about it.

Healthy competition and banter between the salespeople are a good sign of a top performing team. Allocating individual quiet areas too is vital to making sales calls. This is challenging work and the last thing you need is a bank of colleagues listening in on your every word!

But... an aspect of PLACE that is becoming even more important than the physical office space is the VIRTUAL PLACE.

Technology has provided sales with the potential to accelerate performance and productivity exponentially, but how many companies truly realise this and invest wisely to capitalise on the opportunity?

A salesperson today should have real-time access to all their customer history and information, allowing them to rapidly communicate with clients regardless of their physical location. The use of mobile applications that sync automatically with the company's central CRM system allows today's salesperson to be able to update client information from sales calls within 90 seconds.

This speed allows companies to gather vital real-time customer data easily and effectively.

>>>>>>>>>

Using this technology greatly increases the level of adoption by the sales force. Finally, it reduces the labour intensity involved in keeping CRM data up-to-date. Using audio visual platforms like Skype, or GoToMeeting have revolutionised the way sales teams communicate.

Think for a moment, of the impact on sales productivity when you drag 10 sales people off the road for a day to attend a sales meeting?

Compare this to the alternative of joining the team on a live video conference call for an hour of their day, together with the ability to share documents and edit these collaboratively in real time.

By harnessing these three elements, top companies globally are creating high-performance sales cultures that deliver results year in, year out.

CHAPTER 14.

Conclusion

The Four Key Elements to achieve consistent top sales performance

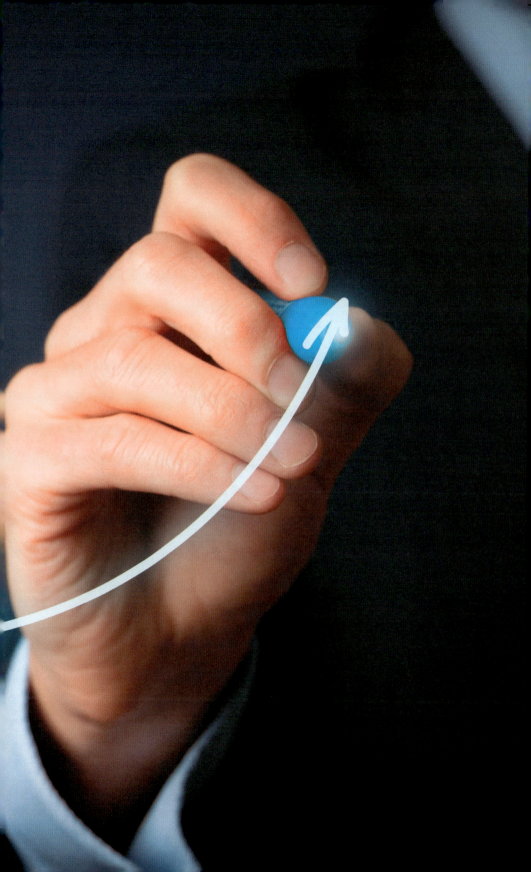

1. RIGHT PEOPLE

Foundational to creating high performance is getting the right team in place. No other activity can substitute for the work done at this initial stage. Creating a professional sales recruitment process will save you hours and hundreds of thousands in revenue. Focus on discovering the qualities that have made salespeople successful in your company or industry. Set about creating a list of the top ones you will look for and identify during the whole interview process. Apart from relevant experience, consider the individual's character. Will they fit into this team and add value?

2. RIGHT MANAGEMENT OVERSIGHT

Once you decide to hire your new salesperson what's next?

- How can you ensure that individual becomes a champion for the business?
- How can your onboarding process save you thousands in recruitment and training costs?
- What would a 10% reduction in staff attrition contribute to the bottom line?

The answers to these questions have much to do with how you use the first 90 days together.

>>>>>>>>>>>

Many companies present the new salesperson with their company manual, mobile phone, and laptop, followed by some basic product and brand training. The new person is then dispatched into the field, only to be reunited again with their manager at the next sales meeting. This formative and highly valuable first three-month period is a topic that receives little attention. However, the impact on staff retention and the bottom line is significant.

Read the article "How crucial are the first 90 days to your success?" for some useful insights.
(www.linearstructure.com/how-crucial-are-the-first-90-days-to-your-success/)

In addition to creating confident new staff who are comfortable and competent, an on-going structured sales management process is required to manage a high-performance sales team. If you'd like to understand more about how these processes can help you gain visibility and control, *please watch the video - The 5 Pillars of Sales Management which clearly explains the value of these process.*
(www.linearstructure.com/insights/videos/)

115

Ultimately by using a collaborative approach with your team, they will grow in proficiency and allow you to maximise their potential.

3. RIGHT METRICS

Selecting the right metrics may at first glance seem a rudimentary affair.

However, research has shown there is, in fact, a great variety when it comes to what the top companies choose to measure and monitor. This is surprising when you consider these companies have decades of sales experience and invest literally millions into their CRM systems. Would you expect to find a clearly defined short list of key sales metrics for the rest of us to implement religiously? Well probably...but that is simply not the case.

It's not uncommon to find companies measuring all kinds of facts and figures simply because they can. In addition, old historic reports will be added to newer ones as new managers join the business. In a short time this reporting can morph into a plethora of data that threatens to drown any sales manager.

I recently worked with a managing director who had an assortment of 25 different multi-colored graphs to demonstrate sales performance! We must stop this insanity and get the data to work for us and not against us.

One way to do this is to cut back. Ask yourself this question.

Why am I measuring this?

The only reason to measure something is because it's linked to the key activities you need to take to achieve your goal, or to check the results you're getting to ensure you are on the right path and enable you to make any needed mid-course correction.

4. RIGHT REWARDS

Setting up the correct commission structure is vital to drive the desired behaviour from the sales team. Often companies treat their commission structure as a separate entity to their sales strategy. They seem oblivious to the strong link between what people do and what they get rewarded for.

I've worked with firms that paid commission even if the salespeople didn't hit their target!

I've seen companies put a cap on earnings where the salespeople were incentivised to literally sit back and relax once they had achieved target three months before the year end!

117

Then, there was the company that surrounded the payment of commission with caveats linked to the company successfully achieving their overall net margin. What do you think this plan did to the sales team's motivation? But most frequently I see companies that are paying their commission based on general or arbitrary KPI's. They're not harnessing the power and energy of their sales teams by directing their behaviour and efforts in the most effective way.

So why not actively encourage the specific behaviours you want to see. Create the reward system that focuses the sales team's time and effort in line with the company's sales strategy.

Fine tuning these four areas takes time, effort and diligence but the payoff in exponential sales growth is well worth the effort.

>>>>>>>>>>

In conclusion, I'd like to thank you for reading these thoughts, insights, and ideas. I encourage you to take the points that resonate with you and start applying them to your team. I believe there has never been a more exciting time to develop yourself and build a strong and resilient high-performance team.

To your continued success.

Peter

Made in the USA
Columbia, SC
29 August 2018